POCKET JAPAN

A CONCISE GUIDEBOOK FOR
BUSINESS TRAVELERS TO JAPAN

JOHN W. FEIST

POCKET JAPAN
A Concise Guidebook for Business Travelers to Japan
Copyright © 2021 by John W. Feist.
All rights reserved.

No part of this publication may be reproduced by photocopying, scanning, or any other means, or stored in a retrieval system, transmitted in any form, or published by any means, without prior written permission of the author, except in the case of attributed, brief quotations embodied in critical articles and reviews.

Inquiries should be addressed to: John W. Feist, 2335 Dale Drive, Falls Church, VA, 22043, USA, or jwfeist@aol.com

ISBN (print): 978-1-7357497-6-1
ISBN (ebook): 978-1-7357497-7-8

Book design by Domini Dragoone.
"Courtesan Scroll" image from the author's collection; all other images sourced from 123rf.com and iStock.com.

PUBLISHED BY

CONTENTS

You're Headed for Japan ~ 1

Preparing for Departure ~ 7

Meeting Preparation ~ 15

Culture ~ 21

Language Hints ~ 29

Hospitality ~ 33

Resources ~ 37

From the Author ~ 47

YOU'RE HEADED FOR JAPAN

Maybe it happens this way: It's a Friday, traffic was a hassle getting in, you've got a full plate already, and there's a message from the CEO. The subject line says, "Japan Trip." You read:

You've been in on the brainstorming, and now I want you on the team to make it happen in Japan. The plan is to leave one month from today. The attached memo has my vision of what we want to achieve and a rough agenda.

Next Tuesday, we're meeting with a couple of cross-cultural trainers for a half-day session. They know their stuff. Any prep you can do on your own after that session would be great. Let me know by Monday if you're in and can clear your decks to be away three weeks.

You are most definitely in and send back a "yes!"

Or, maybe it happens this way: You're the boss, and it's your company, your vision, and your trip.

Either way, *you're headed for Japan.*

The trainers, Evan and Sonoko Patterson, start with some history and practical advice before getting into Japan's business culture and social aspects.

HISTORICAL PERSPECTIVE.
For over two thousand years, the Japanese have both assimilated and resisted foreign influence, mostly that of its Asian neighbors. The Japanese openly and directly emulated Chinese traditions, beginning in the late seventh century, especially in its capital cities, first in Nara and then Kyoto. While Japan successfully repelled occasional invasions from China and Korea, it absorbed Chinese influences such as Buddhism, the tea ceremony, and bureaucracy. Buddhism, the quest for individual enlightenment, co-exists happily today with Japan's native Shinto religion, pantheistic and animistic, which focuses on more practical matters like a good rice harvest, fertility, health, and safe passage on the seas.

From the late twelfth century to the early years of the seventeenth, Japan's warrior clans regularly fought hand-to-hand, blood-soaked civil wars to gain power and dominance over territory. The powerful military ruler Tokugawa Ieyasu subdued and consolidated these warring clans. He concentrated bureaucratic government in Edo—which became Tokyo—while aristocratic trappings and sophistication remained with the Emperor in Kyoto.

During the Edo Period—the two-plus centuries preceding the start of the Meiji Era in 1868—Japan lived in self-imposed isolation from the outside world. This period of seclusion was known as *sakoku*. During this time, Japanese society experienced Western influence only through carefully controlled commerce and trade and the occasional shipwreck.

In 1853, however, Commodore Matthew Perry arrived with a force of ten war vessels and sixteen hundred armed men. A year later, he sealed the open-trade bargain U.S. President Millard Fillmore had demanded, forcing Japan to open up to the rest of the world. Japan's military government was overthrown, and Emperor Meiji relocated sovereign and military power to Edo, which he renamed Tokyo.

As a result of *sakoku* isolation, Japan had never encountered Greek and Roman classicism, the Dark Ages, the Renaissance, the Reformation, or the Enlightenment. Democratic institutions in Japan only date back to the mid-nineteenth century. After that, Japan vaulted from farming and mercantilism directly into industrialization, empire-building, war, devastating defeat, a new constitution in 1947, and the construction of a world-class economy now third only to the United States and China.

In the modern-day, Japan's major urban areas glow with neon and gleaming new buildings. The Japanese themselves look modern and Western in conservative business attire. They assimilate Western technology and medicine, social trends, entertainment, and fashion.

But looks deceive. Their tradition, culture, and history influence their interactions with you, so you'll need to orient yourself—pun intended— to a few basics to see behind the curtain. There are close to 127 million people there, and ninety-nine percent of adults are literate.

Sonoko Patterson takes over the session to discuss some practical matters before you depart.

PREPARING FOR DEPARTURE

PASSPORT, MEDICAL, AND TRAVEL INSURANCE.

Make sure you have a passport, and that it's current. Arrange insurance coverage if your existing health plan does not cover foreign travel, and carry both your insurance policy identity card as proof of insurance and a claim form. Even though some health plans include "customary and reasonable" hospital costs abroad, check whether yours pays for medical evacuation back to the United States (possibly more than $50,000 depending on your location and medical condition). For this, Sonoko suggests "Emergency Assistance Plus," an insurer. High-quality medical treatment by English-speaking medical personnel is available in major urban areas in Japan if necessary. Finally, check the websites in *Resources* for where things stand on the COVID situation, always a moving target.

A PLACE TO START.

If your company already works with a trading company or other ally, that's great. If not, consider using the American Chamber of Commerce in Japan as a contact point and source of information; you'll find a link in the *Resources* section. A Japanese trading company or partner can be invaluable, so long as you pick carefully. BDTI GoToData Service (see *Resources*) is an excellent resource for vetting potential allies.

MISSION.

Since you're traveling to Japan on business, you have a mission. Know the business mission, stick to it, and be prepared to articulate the mission with conviction throughout your stay.

IKIGAI.

Ikigai, a word meaning "reason for being" in Japanese, refers to the values and beliefs that bring joy and purpose to life. By extension, the Japanese organization will have a mission statement, and its employees are schooled and steeped in it. The Mitsubishi Corporation's stated philosophy rests on three principles:

(i) corporate responsibility to society; (ii) integrity and fairness; and (iii) global understanding through business. Research and understand your counterpart's mission statement; you'll find it useful for understanding their corporate culture. For example, if you're at an evening event with toasts, use it to add depth to your toast. The Japanese team will take notice.

CONNECTIVITY.

In preparation for the Olympics and Paralympics, Japan made significant moves to link the population and visitors to the Internet via Wi-Fi on both a national and community level. Virtually every hotel, inn, and Airbnb spot in the nation also offers wireless connectivity, even if only in the lobby. That's in addition to all the restaurants, coffee shops, bars, and other retail businesses hoping to lure in customers. Your hotel probably also makes smartphones available as an amenity. Accordingly, you don't need to rush into buying a SIM card, unless you decide to head out into the countryside.

Check the *Resources* section for a few apps that will allow you to access vast networks of Wi-Fi connections that will ensure you virtually never go dark online.

BUSINESS CARDS (MEISHI).

Be sure to take a large stack of business cards with your info printed on one side in Japanese and English on the other. Always treat the cards you receive as documents worth preserving. When meeting someone, extend your card with two hands as a gesture of respect, and bow slightly. Receive the other person's card in the same way. Look at it. Repeat the person's name and title if you need clarification. If you're in a meeting, array the cards in front of you to organize where the people are seated (which helps you to connect names to faces). After the meeting, store the cards you receive in a case sized for the purpose. Sort this all out before leaving. It makes a huge difference if you are perceived as more sensitive than people who simply stuff the cards they receive in a wallet, pocket, or purse.

Hint: If you can't find a printer locally that handles bilingual print runs, try mojoprint.jp in Japan. They're fast, do quality work, and are extremely reliable.

STATUS, VISIBILITY, CONNECTIONS, AND RELATIONSHIPS.
If you're going to Japan to buy something or invest your company's money, your situation is enviable. If you are going there to sell something or to obtain Japanese financing, you are going there to meet the king, because the Japanese are hardwired to think that the customer is king. And since Japanese consumers are notoriously demanding in terms of quality, it's the perfect market test-bed. Like New York, if you can make it here, you can make it anywhere.

Here's something else to keep in mind when you want to market something in Japan: You may have a superior product or service, offer better terms on price and availability, and even be easy to work with, but Japanese companies and customers may still say no thanks. One big reason for rejection is that unless you're a known quantity and selling well elsewhere abroad, you're inherently considered a risky bet here.

That spotlights the importance of networking and nurturing relationships. How far back relationships go, and the *senpai-kohai* (senior-junior) system are all vital cultural touchpoints. Sonoko Patterson still keeps in contact with people she knew in grade school.

LENGTH OF STAY.

Plan an extended stay, and then build in extra time. How long? If you are the rookie in a group that visits Japan frequently, the schedule will probably be largely decided. If you are leading the team, or are on your own, count on staying for at least two weeks. One of the first things your counterparts will want to discuss will be your schedule—and the date you plan to return home. Don't be breezy and announce you want to wrap things up in three days. You must understand the circle of consensus (discussed below) that your counterpart must deal with before the Japanese side reaches a final decision. As a rule, surprises and sudden appearances and requests are not viewed favorably in Japan, so set up meetings as far in advance as you can.

Sonoko next turns to meeting preparation steps to observe before departure and in-country.

MEETING PREPARATION

PRE-MEETING PREPARATION.

Expect your Japanese counterparts to want to know ahead of time what your meeting will be about. They view the process as *Nemawashi*, or prior consultation, laying the foundation; the term literally means "to prepare the root." The Japanese have a very different way of conducting business meetings. Participants have already drawn conclusions regarding information to be presented before a formal meeting even starts. This system was developed to avoid surprises, discrepancies, and gain agreement from everyone in advance when making a decision in a formal meeting. It is also meant to keep relationships harmonious.

MEETINGS.

When you're in a meeting with more than one individual from a Japanese company, break up your delivery to help accommodate the interpreter. You should never focus all your time, words, and attention on the person who speaks your language best. Chances are that the person who's the quietest in the room—and even appears to be asleep—is the decision-maker in the group. COVID protocols may have altered the meeting surroundings and procedures, but not the underlying business culture we're talking about here.

TEAM COHESIVENESS.

Two connective tissues help hold a Japanese team together: harmony and *on* (obligation).

HARMONY.

American Ambassador Edwin Reischauer wrote, "The key Japanese value is harmony, which they seek to achieve by a subtle process of mutual understanding, almost by intuition, rather than by…clear-cut decisions, whether by dictates or majority votes. Decisions…should not be left up to any one man but should be arrived at by consultations and committee work. Consensus is the goal—a general agreement as to the sense of the meeting, to which no one continues to hold strong objections." (see: *The Japanese*, Reischauer, in *Resources*)

OBLIGATION.

The Japanese word is *on* (sounds like "own"), which expresses a burden to be borne, or more accurately, worn. A person receives the parental *on* of filial piety and continues through life wearing some form of *on* in every successive relationship. Work entangles one in loyalty, obedience, and exchanges of assistance, each carrying an *on*. Think of it as a web of mutual indebtedness. (*Chrysanthemum and the Sword*, Benedict, in *Resources*)

CIRCLE OF CONSENSUS.

The Japanese company is a team, but one with loyalty on steroids. Its members work with one another on the premise that they will be together until retirement, even though "cradle-to-grave" employment was never guaranteed for any but those in major corporations, and much of that has eroded as well. Decision-making is circular and time-consuming, usually accomplished through the use of a document called a *ringisho*. It contains the case for a decision, and it circulates to all who need to sign off by affixing their *hanko* (personal seal). The originator of the *ringisho* shepherds it through the system.

He or she will attempt to have a one-on-one conversation with all key people to convince them of the proposal's merits.

For any given decision, by the way, every member of the Japanese team may ask you a question. Never treat any question as trivial. Rank it as coming from the CEO. Sweet reason and critical thinking are your main tools.

Evan Patterson then turns to the country's social and cultural aspects more generally.

Find beneath Tokyo's neon skin Japan's enduring cultural spirit. It synthesizes life, nature, awareness, art, craft, and respect for interconnectedness. Find it, say, in such a commonplace act as rejoining shards of a dropped porcelain dish. Called *kintsugi*, the process makes no attempt to hide the break lines, but rather uses them as seams of gold in a second act of creation.

CULTURE

POPULATION DENSITY.

Japan's urban areas are packed, and you'll probably feel hemmed in on the streets, trains, and public spaces. Japan's population lives on 30 percent of its landmass, and the concentration of people per square kilometer is 347; in the U.S., it is 36. The whole country could fit within the borders of California. California is the most populous state in America. Its population of about 40 million compares to 38 million of Greater Metropolitan Tokyo.

KINDNESS AND HOSPITALITY.

Density statistics aside, Japan is one of the kindest, most gracious places you will ever visit. Japanese adhere to courtesies and reserve learned from infancy and practiced throughout their lives. The traditional Japanese Shinto belief that everything, including plants and trees, has a spirit has cultivated compassion in many for all living creatures. And when it comes to hospitality, the Japanese are convinced they've taken the concept and its execution to a higher level. There's even a special word for it: *omotenashi*.

CLEANLINESS AND ORDER.

Despite its close-packed population, Japan is a land of order and devotion to minutiae. You'll ride in fastidiously clean taxis and trains. It's one of the visible marks of the meticulous cultural spirit behind the scrubbing and deliberations to which your counterparts will subject your business proposals.

BONDING AND PERSONAL RELATIONSHIPS.

Personal bonds always count in business, but few places value them more than in Japan. If you fail to bond with people on a personal level, your stay in Japan will seem long and fruitless. Examining the culture and language of Japan will reward you. You'll find references to sources of information about Japanese history, language, and culture in the *Resources* section.

FUN.

Bonding also occurs by having fun together, which takes place away from the office. After a long day, you may not feel like a long night with your business counterparts, but they will expect it. If you are ever to see their reserve drop, it will no doubt be during a night out eating and drinking (or on a golf course), COVID restrictions permitting.

PUNCTUALITY.

Japan takes time management very seriously. Japanese children learn the importance of punctuality from a young age at school. Office workers arrive at meetings at least five minutes before the scheduled start time to get settled. The trains depart and arrive at stations consistently on time. At peak hours, there are thirteen bullet trains per hour traveling in each direction on the busiest of nine lines. Each train, with a minimum headway of three minutes between trains, arrives and departs on time to the minute.

There's no wiggle room here. Japanese regard punctuality as a mark of reliability and a reflection of your personality. Be on time, period. Check the *Resources* section for the Japan Transit Planner app, which will make this much easier to accomplish.

BOWING.

The Japanese appreciate any effort you make at reflecting their culture. A handshake is universal, but learning how to bow is a social grace that's easy to learn and will win you some serious respect. The Pattersons demonstrate and then recommend a good tutorial: https://gogonihon.com/en/blog/japanese-bow.

FACE.

It starts with a smile. Remember the Japanese expression about first impressions: "He has a good face." You want them to feel that way about you. A good face is open and sincere.

LOSS OF FACE.

In Japan and China, in particular, face also refers to status, respect, and integrity. "Loss of face" means embarrassment, and it is deeply wounding. Do not cause your counterparts to lose face, such as loudly disagreeing with them in public. There is virtually always a way to work around a dilemma without loss of face, so look for it.

CONTROLLED EMOTIONS.

Politeness and reserve predominate over-emotional outbursts or anger. Dignity means blending in, not standing out. If you can match this attitude, you will be rewarded and form bonds. Lonely Planet's guide to Japan describes the Japanese as: "… a people who highly value group identity and smooth social harmony—in a tightly packed city or small farming village, there simply isn't room for colorful individualism. One of the ways of preserving harmony is by forming consensus and concealing personal opinions and true feelings."

STUBBORNNESS, ARROGANCE, AND OTHER BAD BEHAVIOR.

Not all is tranquility or harmony in the spirits of some Japanese individuals. "The Japanese are…both aggressive and unaggressive… insolent and polite, rigid and adaptable, submissive, and resentful of being pushed around, loyal, and treacherous. Both the sword and the chrysanthemum are part of the picture." (Ruth Benedict in *Resources*)

Expect that somewhere along the line, you'll confront an arrogant or stubborn person that threatens to disrupt the way to "yes." If you sense it, all others on the Japanese side have picked up the same thing and have lived with it for years. If you deal with it deftly and with grace, everyone will take notice and respect you for it. Resist the urge to confront arrogance with arrogance. Find a way to higher ground. Find a way to let the Japanese need for harmony resolve the outlier's disruption.

Even though politeness, dignity, self-effacement, and conformity are general rules, there are disturbing exceptions. A Japanese psychologist coined *pawahara* (power harassment) to describe supervisor bullying, growing to the extent that new legislation requires Japanese firms to establish anti-harassment procedures. Groping, a crime in Japan wherever committed, became prevalent on subways to such an extent that one or two female-only cars are now available on subway trains.

Next, Sonoko Patterson points out useful phrases and their meanings.

LANGUAGE HINTS

She also suggests using a few of the online apps mentioned in the *Resources* section—Google Translate, Learn Japanese-Phrasebook for Travel in Japan, and Lingvanex Translator—which all offer audible pronunciation guides.

Hajimemashite. "Nice to meet you," gets you started on the right foot.

Yoroshiku onegaishimasu is a convenient way to end conversations on a forward-looking note. It means something along the lines of "I'll do my best going forward."

Arigato. "Thank you" is your best friend among Japanese phrases.

Sumimasen. "Excuse me" is your next best friend, whether to catch someone's attention or apologize for stepping on her toe.

Konnichiwa. "Good afternoon," but also just "Good day."

Hai. This word does not always mean "yes"; it is an acknowledgment that the listener has heard you. It's closer to "I get it," or "I understand what you're saying," so be sure to clarify if you must hear actual assent or commitment.

Iie. This means "no," but is used rarely and selectively, so listen for negation in expressions of evasion or equivocation and watch body language.

Wakarimashita and *wakarimasen.* "I understand"; "I don't understand."

HOSPITALITY

DOWNTIME PLANNING.
Count on having downtime, and use this time to dip into the culture. The concierge in your hotel is the best resource for ideas and reservations, but there are others in print and online noted in the *Resources* section. Consider exploring Japan's unique forms of theater, for example, Kabuki, Noh, and Bunraku (puppets). Sophie Richard's *Guide* is valuable for finding museums, also in the *Resources* section. The Idemitsu Museum of Arts, near the Imperial Palace in the center of Tokyo, is a wondrous place well worth a look.

CULTURAL SPIRIT.
The Embassy of Japan's website states: "Traditional cultural arts often embody the values of *wabi* (elegant stillness) and *sabi* (antiquated elegance with calm)." Think carefully about this succinct description; it contains two millennia of insight into the

people you will be meeting. You can see examples in museums and even in the displays of large department stores.

DEPARTMENT STORES.

Department stores play a much more central role in Japanese life than in the West. Only the best quality products are on sale here, and at prices to match. You can think of a depato as an art gallery as well as a shop. They typically have a food floor that offers samples of various delicacies.

GET OUT OF TOWN.

If you are stuck over a weekend, take a train somewhere. Consult the concierge. Head off to Hakone, Nikko, or Kyoto for a glimpse of nature and old Japan. Take an overnight bag and try a *ryokan* (traditional inn) or *onsen* (hot spring).

RECIPROCAL ENTERTAINMENT.

When you think about hosting an evening for your counterparts, consider something with a local flair. The hotel concierge can help you. Take them somewhere featuring *robatayaki* (farm/country-style grill), for example, where everyone will quickly loosen up.

GIFTS.
Don't be caught short-handed when it comes to gifts for your counterparts. High-end food items in individually packed portions are a welcome present.

END OF TRIP.
You do have a gift to take home, right? If you have excess currency, keep some for the next trip. A handwritten thank-you note to your counterparts will put a fitting end to the journey.

At the end of the session, the Pattersons hand everyone on the away team a curated list of resources and websites.

RESOURCES

A COVID COMPASS.

In October 2022, Japan reopened entry for independent travelers who have been vaccinated. However, COVID precautions and ease of entry are moving targets. Plan well in advance by checking some of the following websites:

- www.Japan.travel

- www.mofa.go.jp (and scroll to "Information on the Novel Corona Virus Diseases")

- https://jp.usembassy.gov/covid-19-information

The 1918 Spanish flu pandemic affected at least 23 million Japanese. The mask culture instituted as a by-product attached itself to a broader, do-the-right-thing etiquette, and the practice has continued ever since. Thus, a cultural (not governmental) imperative prevailed through the COVID pandemic and you can expect widespread mask-wearing everywhere. Unmasked foreigners will be conspicuous and will cause discomfort among the people you deal with.

WEBSITES, BLOGS, AND ORGANIZATIONS.

METROPOLIS MAGAZINE
http://www.metropolisjapan.com
To see what events, entertainment, restaurants, and bars one of the world's greatest cities has to offer, check out this magazine. (Also in print form as a quarterly.)

JAPAN NATIONAL TOURISM ORGANIZATION
https://www.jnto.go.jp
This comprehensive site showcases the best of Japan in over two thousand pages.

BENTO.COM
Eating out in Tokyo, Osaka, Kyoto, Kobe, Nara, Nagoya, or Kanazawa? Then consult this site to find out where to go and for what delicacies. There are sister sites about craft beer, for example.

JAPAN TODAY
https://japantoday.com
Japan Today is a reliable source of up-to-date insights and news on the country.

THE AMERICAN CHAMBER OF COMMERCE IN JAPAN

www.accj.or.jp

Whether you're American or not, the ACCJ is a valued source of information on doing business in Japan. That includes what issues are hot in terms of trade and commerce, social issues such as the status of women in business, and white papers about them. It's also a place to make great contacts on the ground and seek out possible partners for alliances.

U.S. STATE DEPARTMENT

www.travel.state.gov

Helpful for notes and alerts on international travel, emergency contacts, and more.

CARTERJMRN BLOG

https://www.carterjmrn.com/blog

CarterJMRN is a well-respected market research firm in Tokyo that puts out articles on consumer trends, which also delve into Japan's national psyche from several perspectives: generational dynamics, internationalization, the changing world of work and women power.

APPS.

LEARN JAPANESE—PHRASEBOOK FOR TRAVEL IN JAPAN
https://apps.apple.com/us/app/learn-japanese-phrasebook-for-travel-in-japan/id447047877

(Codegent), iPhone/iPod/iPad app; the basic version is free. This app has twenty-one categories for various greetings, times and dates, transportation and so on, and will say the phrases for you and slow down the audio if you want. You can also copy and paste text to find out what it means.

JAPAN TRANSIT PLANNER
https://world.jorudan.co.jp/mln/en/?sub_lang=nosub

A great free tool for getting around the country, Japan Transit Planner shows times, alternate routes, fares, and modes of transport. Available via P.C. and as a smartphone app.

NHK WORLD
[Public television] disaster app; download the English version.

JAPAN CONNECTED-FREE WI-FI

A smartphone app that lets you register for access to around 200,000 free tourist hotspots offered by numerous companies and organizations. You'll need to submit some personal data to join.

FREE WI-FI PASSPORT

This passport provides free access to around 400,000 Softbank hotspots at major train stations, hotels, restaurants, cafés, and other locations all over Japan. You'll need to call a toll-free number from a foreign cellphone while connected to the Softbank network to get your password.

GOOGLE TRANSLATE

Stuck on a stubborn language point? Use Google Translate to find the Japanese you're looking for, and its camera function to do a quick-and-dirty translation of text. You can also use it to get pronunciations of words and phrases.

LINGVANEX TRANSLATOR

https://lingvanex.com
(NordicWise Limited) If you'd like to work beyond the relative confines of Google

Translate, try Lingvanex Translator. This robust translation and dictionary app lets you read, write, and even speak over 110 different languages (including Japanese). And Lingvanex doesn't just handle documents in a variety of formats—it also translates voice, text in images, websites, and documents. Even better, it works on multiple platforms, including Windows, MacOS, iOS, and Android.

BDTI GOTODATA SERVICE
www.bdti.or.jp/en
(The Board Director Training Institute of Japan) If you need to make a deep info-dive on a potential Japanese partner, look at GoToData. This service combines A.R. financials, basic financial data, corporate governance reports, and AGM voting results processed through an A.I. into English. GoToData offers data on over 3,500 TSE1, TSE2, JASDAQ, and MOTHERS firms—all listed firms. Through this service, you can gain data few foreign firms have access to in English because so few Japanese companies issue this info—fewer than one in ten. Even better, this data is updated regularly, and you can spot trends and changes, cut and paste

text and tables, analyze whole industries, and create interactive market reports.

BOOKS AND MAGAZINES.

Lonely Planet Japan, Chris Rowthorn, and others (Lonely Planet Publications, latest print edition August 2019); https://www.lonelyplanet.com/japan. Also available on Kindle.

Tokyo: A Biography, Stephen Mansfield (Tuttle, 2016). Also available on Kindle. The story of Tokyo, built, burned and rebuilt, battered by earthquakes and bombs, only to rise again.

Tokyo's Mystery Deepens, Michael Pronko (Raked Gravel Press, 2014). Here's a series of contemplative essays on life in Tokyo written by a jazz-loving journalist who's worked for Newsweek Japan, Nippon Television, and Artscape Japan.

The Art Lover's Guide to Japanese Museums, Sophie Richard (The Japan Society, 2014). This specialist in Japanese culture delivers personal and compelling introductions to over a hundred of Japan's world-class museums. You'll be able to navigate them with ease with this as your guide.

The Japanese, Edwin Reischauer (Belknap Press of Harvard University Press, 1977). One of the best modern observers of Japan—and a former ambassador to the country—Reischauer distilled his thoughts on Japan and its people into this book. The Japanese admired him greatly and acknowledged the accuracy and humanity of his insights.

The Chrysanthemum and the Sword, Ruth Benedict (Riverside Press, 1946). American anthropologist Ruth Benedict never actually lived in Japan. However, her classic summary of the country's culture based on history, social structures, and literature still retains significant validity despite being written right after World War II.

The World Turned Upside Down: Medieval Japanese Society, Pierre Souyri (trans. Käthe Roth, Columbia University Press, 2001). Souyri's engaging style brings Japan's medieval period from the late twelfth century to the Warring States Period to life. The bloody conflicts of powerful feudal clans, new forms of cultural expression, and other aspects of the turbulent centuries are sketched in vivid strokes.

Step Up, Leland Gaskins (Intuition Press, 2019; print and Kindle editions available). In *Step Up*, Leland Gaskins addresses common cross-cultural differences between Japanese and Western businesspeople from the standpoint of a young Japanese employee at a foreign firm. He has to deal with expectations based on a different work culture and resolve them to keep his career. The knowledge he gains can be applied in reverse by Western businesspeople. Gaskins has been an executive in the investment and education fields for over two decades.

Japan: A Personal Memoir, Roger Pulvers (Balestier Press, 2020). Originally published in Japanese, this book mixes aspects of history, culture, and everyday life. He illuminates the inventive elements that have made Japanese culture and design the envy of the world.

FROM THE AUTHOR

I've traveled to Japan as a lawyer for steel, coal, cement, and shipping companies as part of business teams that successfully negotiated significant, long-term transactions. This guidebook draws on what I've seen and experienced during more than thirty business trips there, and what I've read and researched. When I'm not at home in Falls Church, Virginia, I visit Japan frequently to gather material for my novels—more about which on the next page and www.johnwfeist.com.

I am deeply indebted to Doug Jackson for contributions to this guidebook. Doug lives in Tokyo, where he heads up Fresh Eyes Communications (www.fresheyes.jp). A longtime editor, published author, and columnist, Doug has over four decades of communications and media experience in the U.S. and Japan, including six years as the communications director of the American Chamber of Commerce in Japan.

FINAL TIPS.

"International business travel" is a misnomer. Better might be, "International business hurry-up-and-wait." So, take along a good read, or three. Here're some ideas; I know the author. All are on Amazon in paperback, ebook, and Audible audiobook formats.

Night Rain, Tokyo (2017). Is it a compelling idea or just wishful thinking? Brad Oaks pursues a radical international trade proposal that would rescue a family steel business and secure a scarce natural resource for America. Someone with a sniper's rifle is clearly against the deal. Brad tracks down a previously unknown heir to the business, and both become profoundly entangled in this suspenseful, fast-paced political thriller right out of tomorrow's newspapers.

Blind Trust (2019). "A unique and satisfying geopolitical thriller set in the cultural trappings of the Land of the Rising Sun. Recommended." Chanticleer Reviews (five stars); blue-ribbon award winner, Chanticleer International Book Awards, suspense, and thriller division. Tokyo's lights go dark, and the bullet trains stop running. What good can come of a nationwide power outage? Steel executive Brad Oaks and wife Amaya put their family planning on hold to answer that question and help her friend, Yuko Kagono, Japan's first female prime minister. *Blind Trust* reunites characters from *Night Rain, Tokyo,* and introduces dynamic new players.

Doubt and Debt (2021). Brad Oaks' best friend wants him to help enemies of the United States. A voracious corporate raider wants to take over his family's business. And an unknown adversary wants him, his wife and daughter dead. Follow battles of wits and wiles as they unfold in this political and romantic suspense thriller, sequel to *Blind Trust*.

Ship of Perils (2022). The Speaker of the House of Representatives will sink someone's ship or he'll be sunk by his own ethics breach. The prime minister of Japan needs help on a secret mission. Brad and Amaya Oaks get drawn into the undertow of both perils while their daughter goes off to lobby for gun reform. Buffeted by winds from these storms, can the family even stay afloat?

www.ingramcontent.com/pod-product-compliance
Lightning Source LLC
Chambersburg PA
CBHW040109120526
44589CB00040B/2832